A Robbie Reader

Going to School

AROUND THE WORLD

Melissa
Koosmann

Mitchell Lane
PUBLISHERS
P.O. Box 196
Hockessin, Delaware 19707
Visit us on the web: www.mitchelllane.com
Comments? email us: mitchelllane@mitchelllane.com

Mitchell Lane
PUBLISHERS

Meet Our New Student From

Australia • China • Colombia • Great Britain
• Haiti • India • Israel • Japan • Korea • Malaysia •
Mali • Mexico • New Zealand • Nicaragua • Nigeria
• Quebec • South Africa • Tanzania • Zambia •
Going to School Around the World

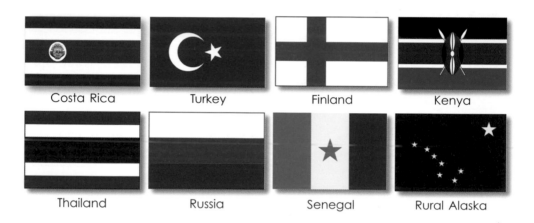

Costa Rica   Turkey   Finland   Kenya

Thailand   Russia   Senegal   Rural Alaska

Printing   1   2   3   4   5   6   7   8   9

**Library of Congress
Cataloging-in-Publication Data**

Koosman, Melissa.
  Going to school around the world / By Melissa Koosman.
    p. cm. — (A Robbie reader)
  Includes bibliographical references and index.
  ISBN 978-1-58415-782-3 (library bound)
  1. Schools—Cross-cultural studies—Juvenile literature. I. Title.
  LB1556.K66 2010
  372—dc22
                         2009027348

                                PLB

CONTENTS

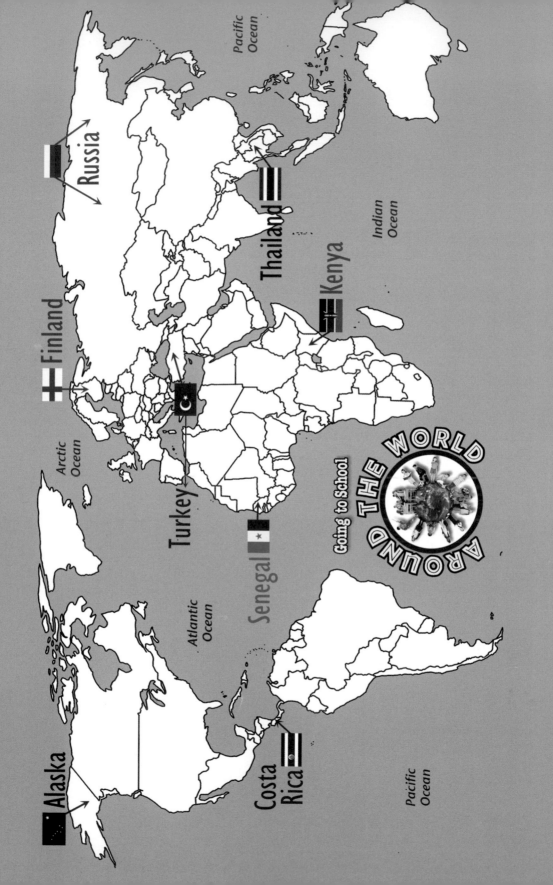

Introduction

The students in this book are not real people, but their stories show what life is really like for some children in other countries as they go to school. You will read about how kids get to school in the morning, what they study, what games they play at recess, and so on. The characters live all around the globe, in big cities and tiny villages. They belong to different races, cultures, and religions. Some have many opportunities to succeed, and others have very few.

As I researched this book, I found small, colorful differences between cultures I would never have imagined. I also noticed similarities I didn't expect. I hope you will be surprised in the same way. How many kids in this book ride to school in a school bus? How many have to learn math? How many greet their teachers in a different way than you do?

This book describes only one school for each country it covers. Because of this, it does not tell you about the many differences that exist within each country. The chapter about Kenya would be a different story if it were about a big city school instead of a small village school. In the same way, the United States school in this book is probably unlike the school you go to.

Although it could not possibly include everything about every country, I hope the book will show you that the customs, wealth, and values of each country have a huge effect on the lives of the students who live there. Everything from what they wear to school to whether they go to school at all depends partly on the accident of where they were born. This goes for you, too. How does your country affect you? How might your life be different if you were born in another place?

This book would not have been possible without the help of many people around the world who agreed to be interviewed for these stories, many of whom provided photographs. You can read more about them on page 60.

Costa Rica

Dense rain forest surrounds the two large craters of the Poas Volcano in Costa Rica. The area is a popular tourist attraction near Costa Rica's capital, San José.

Costa Rica

Chapter

Gabriel whistled as he kicked his soccer ball down the street. The walk to school wasn't far, and he was early, so he didn't hurry.

Suddenly, somebody ran up behind him and kicked the ball away from him.

"Antonio!" shouted Gabriel. "Cut it out."

Antonio dribbled the ball, grinning. Gabriel didn't bother trying to steal it back. Antonio was the best soccer player in the school.

"Oh, fine. Here you go," Antonio said. He kicked the ball back to Gabriel. The boys made a game of passing it back and forth as they walked. When they arrived at the school, a couple of other kids joined their game. The playground was wet from recent rain, so their blue school uniform pants got muddy around the cuffs.

Too soon, the principal clapped her hands to signal that the day was about to begin. The students gathered in lines on the playground and sang the Costa Rican national anthem. Then the principal began the announcements.

"Next week we'll celebrate Children's Day," she said. "Our school will put on our own Olympic games."

The kids cheered, and the principal took a bow. "Each class has a job to do to prepare for our Olympics. I want you all to help."

She clapped her hands again, and Gabriel and Antonio walked with the other 23 kids in their class to their third-grade room. The school was made up of three concrete buildings for classrooms,

Students in Gabriel's school compete in a wheelbarrow race at their informal Olympic games. They do not wear their uniforms on this special day.

as well as separate buildings for the kindergarten and cafeteria. The buildings were connected by covered walkways.

The kids in Gabriel's class chatted excitedly about the Olympics. They had trouble standing still by their desks. Their teacher waited for them to get quiet before he greeted them.

"Good morning, class," he said.

"Good morning, teacher," the class responded in **unison** (YOO-nih-sun). They sat down.

"I know you're all excited about the Olympics," the teacher said. "And I'll talk to you about our job in art class at the end of the day. But we need to focus on our studies first."

Gabriel slowly got out his notebook and began to copy the social studies lesson from the board. He hated copying because it made his hand cramp, but the school couldn't afford social studies books. Luckily, the school gave kids textbooks for most of the other classes, including math, science, English, and humanities. They didn't use books for art, PE, or Christian religion. Classes were taught in Spanish.

Every now and then, Gabriel paused and looked around the room. The walls were decorated with a colorful rain forest theme, including animals and palm trees, and a large chalkboard hung at the front. The windows were just holes in the wall with bars across them. This allowed air to flow through and cool the room. Most of the other students scratched away at their notebooks, but Maria and Jessica whispered together.

Gabriel's class works on an art project. The students share pens and other materials because some of them do not have enough.

"Maria! Jessica! Quiet down," warned the teacher.

"Sorry, teacher," the girls said.

Gabriel leaned back over his work. He did okay in school, but he didn't always try his hardest. His parents sometimes said he should put in more effort, or it wouldn't be worth paying his admission fees and buying his uniform. But Gabriel knew they would make sure he graduated from elementary school. Some kids in Gabriel's town weren't so lucky. They dropped out early to work and help support their families.

When the class was dismissed for recess, Gabriel ran outside and joined another soccer game. Some kids jumped rope or played tag, and a few bought snacks from the **soda** (SOH-dah) across the street. When the twenty-minute recess was over, the

If they have money to spare, Gabriel and his friends buy snacks or sweets from a small shop called a *soda*.

students lined up to rinse their muddy shoes at an outdoor sink before they went back inside.

During math, Gabriel's attention drifted. As usual, Maria and Jessica couldn't stop whispering and giggling. The teacher ended up giving both of them pink slips for their parents to sign that evening.

School lunch

At lunch, the kids went to the cafeteria. The food was the same every day: rice and beans and a salad. The kids ate hungrily. Gabriel knew some of them didn't get enough to eat outside of school, so they really needed the free lunch the school gave them.

Art was the final lesson of the afternoon. The teacher smiled and said, "Now let's talk about our Olympic games." He explained that their class had to make gold, silver, and bronze medals out of cardboard. The group quickly got to work cutting circles of cardboard and painting them.

"This is going to be so great," said Gabriel.

"I bet our class will beat the fifth graders in soccer," Antonio said.

Before they knew it, it was time to clean up. It was a Friday, so everyone had to pitch in to rake the playground and pick up garbage before they were dismissed to go home. Gabriel grabbed his notebook with the lessons he had to learn, picked up his soccer ball, and waved to Antonio.

"I have to get home and help in the garden," he said. "Will you have time to play this weekend?"

Children celebrate Costa Rica's Independence Day, September 15, by performing in a parade.

"I'm not sure," said Antonio. "My father is out of town, so I might have to help with the farm animals. Stop by and I'll let you know, okay?"

"Okay." Gabriel tossed his ball to the ground and dribbled it toward home. It wasn't often that they had special activities at school. Next week's Olympics were going to be great. He imagined dodging another player and kicking the ball to score. "Gooooooal!" he yelled.

"Gabriel!" His mother's voice snapped him out of his daydream.

"Coming!" he shouted. He picked up the ball and ran the rest of the way home. For now, games would have to wait.

Make Your Own Rain Forest Palm Tree

You Will Need
A paper towel roll
A paper plate
Scissors
Glue
Brown paint
A brown pen or crayon
Green construction paper
An adult to help you

Instructions

1. Paint the paper towel roll brown. Set it aside to dry.

2. Cut green construction paper into small oval shapes. Use scissors to cut small slits in the sides of the ovals so that they look like palm leaves. You will need about 5-10 leaves.

3. When your paper towel roll is dry, use your pen or crayon to draw short squiggly lines on the roll. This will make it look textured, like bark.

4. Cut one-inch slits into the bottom of the paper towel roll. Fold the slits inward and apply glue to them. Then press the roll firmly to the middle of your paper plate. The plate will form a base so that your tree will stand up.

5. Using a little glue at the bottom of each leaf, glue the leaves into the inside of the top end of the paper towel roll. Let them fan out around the top to complete your tree.

Turkey

Hot-air balloons float over the Cappadocia region of Turkey. The natural rock pillars create a stunning view.

Turkey

Chapter 2

Berna shifted the weight of her heavy schoolbag on her shoulder as she boarded the bus. An old woman with a bag of groceries followed her up the steps. Berna took a seat near the front and watched out the window for her friend Selin. Before the bus stopped, Berna caught sight of Selin's navy blue school uniform. It was identical to the one Berna wore.

"Hi," Selin said, hopping up the steps and plunking herself down next to her friend. The two girls joked around until Berna looked outside and saw a small, barefoot boy in ragged clothes. He was gathering cans by the side of the road.

"I wonder if his school starts later," Berna said.

"He can't be going to school," said Selin. "No uniform."

Berna frowned. Turkey had free public schools, but Berna knew that a small number of kids never went to them. They had to earn money instead. Berna, whose parents paid for private school, was luckier than most.

The bus stopped a few blocks away from the blue concrete school building, and Berna and Selin hopped off. It was a Monday, so the girls made their way to the main yard, where they lined up with the other kids. One of the teachers raised the Turkish flag, and the students sang the national anthem. After this brief ceremony (SAYR-uh-moh-nee), everyone made their way to class. They would sing the anthem again and lower the flag on Friday, when school was over for the week.

Chapter 2

Berna and her classmates wear uniforms to school. They attend a private school, but even public school children in Turkey wear uniforms.

In her classroom, Berna carefully took her schoolbooks out of her bag. The books were expensive, and she knew her parents wanted her to keep them in good shape so that her younger sisters could use them when they got to third grade, too.

Miss Otaran entered the room, and the 21 kids in Berna's class stood up. Miss Otaran greeted the students and told them to sit. As always, the class began the morning by reading newspapers.

At the end of the hour, Miss Otaran asked, "Who is my classroom assistant this week?"

"I am, my teacher," said Berna, addressing Miss Otaran in the polite way all students used.

Miss Otaran pointed at a stack of papers on her desk. "Please hand back last week's homework for me."

"Yes, my teacher," said Berna. She walked around the classroom, distributing papers to each student. The walls of the room were

decorated with posters and the letters of the alphabet. At the front of the room, above the chalkboard, hung a picture of Attaturk, the founder of the Turkish Republic. Berna knew that nobody was allowed to hang anything higher than Attaturk's picture.

Miss Otaran began the math lesson. The other subjects Berna and her classmates studied included Turkish grammar, science, English, and social studies. They also took art, music, and technology classes. When they got older, they would add classes on the Muslim religion and another foreign language.

Miss Otaran worked the students hard, assigning homework in almost every subject. Selin made a face at Berna when Miss Otaran gave them the third assignment of the day. Berna nodded and rolled her eyes. Then she caught herself, remembering the ragged boy she had seen that morning. She enjoyed school, and she knew she was lucky, but it was hard to feel grateful for homework.

Between each lesson, the students were allowed to take a ten- or fifteen-minute break. Lunch recess lasted fifty minutes. Kids could eat snacks from home during breaks, and at lunch they went to the cafeteria. They bought soup, a main dish, and a salad. Today's main dish was a spicy lamb meatball called **kofta** (KOOF-tuh).

Kofta

The teachers often ate in the cafeteria with the students, but not during the Muslim holy month of **Ramadan** (RAH-muh-dahn). During Ramadan, adults didn't eat any food or drink any water during daylight hours. At night, they broke this **fast** and feasted and celebrated. Berna looked forward to Ramadan every year. Because she was only eight, she didn't have to take part in the fasting yet, but she did get to stay up late to enjoy the parties.

Sometimes the kids at Berna's school went on field trips to the theater. On other days, authors or police officers visited the schools to give talks to the students. Berna's class didn't do anything that special today, but Berna had fun making a **mosaic** (moh-ZAY-ik) in art. The kids were just cleaning up the art materials when the vice principal came in. As soon as they noticed her, the students went back to their desks and stood, facing the front of the room.

The vice principal waited until everybody was in place. She winked at Mustafa, a very active boy who sometimes got sent to her office when he misbehaved. Mustafa blushed.

"It looks like you're cleaning right now," the vice principal said, "so I won't rate the neatness of your classroom until you're done. I'll come back after I finish with all the others."

Berna and the other students rushed to finish their jobs. The school held a contest between classrooms to see who could keep theirs the cleanest. Berna's class always seemed to come in last. For once it was nice to know ahead of time that the room was going to be checked.

When the vice principal returned, she nodded in approval. "This is the nicest I've ever seen your room," she said. "I think your class wins for the week."

Miss Otaran looked thrilled as she dismissed the class.

"Want to come to my house and play computer games?" Selin asked as she and Berna waited for the bus home. Around them, their classmates headed off to sports clubs or soccer games. Others went home to watch TV or do chores.

Turkish folk dancers

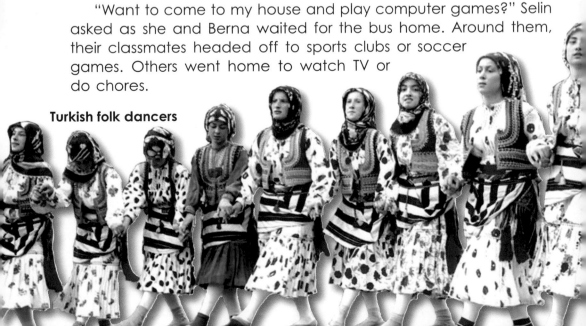

Berna bit her lip. "I want to, but I don't have time."

She lugged her heavy bag onto the bus, thinking about everything she needed to do. She had to help watch her younger sisters while her mother cooked dinner, and her homework would take two or three hours. When Selin hopped off the bus alone, Berna sighed.

As she got out at her stop, Berna saw somebody wave. It was the boy she'd seen that morning gathering cans. He picked up a coin from the road and grinned. Berna smiled back. Suddenly, her schoolbag didn't feel quite so heavy.

Make Your Own Turkish Mosaic

You Will Need
Multicolored construction paper
Scissors
Glue
An adult to help you

In Turkey, artists rarely make pictures of people or animals. Instead, they make colorful mosaics of plants or geometric (jee-oh-MEH-trik) designs. The designs often use blue and white as their main colors, with some reds, greens, and yellows included as well.

Instructions
1. Choose 3 to 5 colors of construction paper. Cut each sheet into shapes about one inch wide. Cut one color into squares, another into triangles, another into diamonds or circles, and so on.

2. Arrange your colored shapes into a design of your choice. You can make it look like a tree or vine; or like a circle, triangle, or other geometric shape.

3. When you've made the design you want, glue the pieces into place on a whole sheet of paper.

Finland

The Suomenlinna Fortress near Helsinki, Finland, was built in 1748. Today it is a World Heritage Site.

Finland

Chapter 3

As soon as the driver came to a stop, Matti hopped off the public bus and dashed toward the school. He ran into the concrete building and up to the second floor. For the millionth time, he wished that the elevator were not reserved for teachers only. He zoomed past the library and entered his classroom. As usual, he made it to his desk just as the bell was ringing.

"How come you never take an earlier bus?" asked Toni.

Matti leaned over, putting his hands on the knees of his jeans as he caught his breath. He felt too silly to tell Toni the real reason. "I just don't want to," he said.

He dropped into his chair, unzipping his schoolbag to get out his homework and his extra pencils. School was free in Finland. Along with textbooks and materials, the school provided one pencil and one eraser per student at the beginning of the year. Matti always lost his in the first week, so he had to bring more from home.

"Good morning, class," said their teacher.

The 19 kids in Matti's class replied in unison: "Good morning, teacher." During this formal greeting, and when they were in trouble, kids usually called their teacher by his title. At other times, they used his first name, Ville (VEE-leh).

As usual, Ville didn't waste any time beginning the school day. He collected the homework and began the science lesson. Matti didn't like science much, or math either, but he liked Finnish

A Finnish teacher hands out rulers for her class to use during a math assignment. Most Finnish children do not wear uniforms to school.

language and literature. He also enjoyed English, and he looked forward to learning Swedish and another language when he got to high school. They would take computer classes in high school, too. Matti loved computers, but in the third grade, only the teacher got to have a computer in the classroom. Besides the core subjects, Matti's class studied PE, music, and arts and crafts. They also studied religion, learning about the religion their parents chose.

At recess, all the kids had to go outside, which was okay with Matti. He kicked a soccer ball around with some other boys. The playground was filled with rocks and trees, which made the game challenging. Often the ball went bouncing off in the wrong direction. There was a jungle gym as well, but Matti preferred soccer. Just as the game was getting good, the bell rang to signal the end of the break.

In arts and crafts, the class made colored snowflakes. They folded coffee filters and cut them into snowflake patterns. Then they dyed them with food coloring. The results didn'l look realistic, but Ville said they'd make the classroom look cheery and colorful during the coming winter. They would go well with the brightly colored posters and student work that covered the walls.

After art, it was Matti's and Toni's turn to tidy the classroom. They cleaned the blackboards and opened the windows. It took so long to scrub the food coloring off the desks that the boys missed the next fifteen-minute recess. Matti wished he'd had the chance to run around a little bit. He squirmed in his seat all through religion, and he kept turning around to see what Toni was writing.

"Matti, I've asked you twice to keep your eyes on your own work," said Ville. "If I have to ask again, I'll send you to see the principal."

"Sorry, teacher." After that, Matti did his best to sit still. Thankfully, the bell rang for lunch a few minutes later. Matti slipped into the back of the cafeteria line. That day's hot food was spaghetti. He chose brown bread and fruit salad to go with it, and the teachers made sure he took milk, too. The city paid for the lunches, so the food was free for all the kids.

Sometimes school seemed pretty humdrum, but there were exciting days, too. When winter came, they would have Athletic Day. The kids would all go skiing and hold a mock winter Olympic games. Matti skied pretty well, but his favorite winter sport was ice hockey. To keep in shape for it, he did a lot of running. That was why he always took the last bus possible to get to school in the mornings—

Cardamom

During Finland's cold winters, people can take reindeer sleigh rides for fun.

so that he'd have to sprint to class. In the afternoons, he jogged all the way home.

When he got home, Matti's T-shirt was covered in sweat. He figured he deserved a break. He switched on his computer and played a few games.

"Turn that off, Matti," said his dad. "Time to do your homework."

"But I just started!" Matti protested.

"Finish your homework, and then you can play more."

Grumbling a little, Matti did as he was told. Luckily, all he had to do was some reading for Finnish. It only took about fifteen

minutes, and he had time to play a while longer before his dad called him down for dinner.

"How was your day?" his dad asked as Matti sat down to eat.

"Not bad," Matti said. "I think I'll do it again tomorrow."

Make Your Own Colored Snowflakes

You Will Need
Old newspapers
Several white coffee filters
Scissors
Food coloring
Tape
String (optional)
An adult to help you

Instructions
1. Spread newspapers over your work surface.

2. Fold a coffee filter in half three times, so that it forms a wedge.

3. Using the scissors, cut small holes and slits into the wedge. If you cut different shapes, you can make each snowflake look different.

4. Carefully squeeze a few very small drops of food coloring onto your wedge.

5. Unfold your coffee filter wedge to see your colored snowflake. Lay it out to dry for a few minutes.

6. Repeat the process to make as many snowflakes as you want. When you're finished, use tape and maybe some string to hang your snowflakes on a wall or in a window.

Traditional Lapland clothing

Kenya

A malachite kingfisher rests on a branch at Lake Nakuru National Park in Kenya. Kenya is home to a wide diversity of bird life.

Kenya

Chapter

Mildred plopped down under the **neem tree** on the playground and sighed. She put on her school uniform shoes, which she always carried from home. It was easier to walk to school barefoot, so her shoes didn't fill with sand. Besides, school shoes were expensive, and this saved them from extra wear.

"Hi, Mildred," said Carol, running over and sitting down beside her friend. The shade of the neem tree was a popular spot. During the dry season, when the classroom got too hot to bear, teachers sometimes brought their classes outside to study under this tree. Even now, during the rainy season, kids flocked to it as a spot to play or to sit and chat before school.

"What's our job today?" asked Mildred.

"Teacher says we're on bathroom duty."

Mildred wrinkled her nose. "Do you think we can trick Ali into trading with us?" She nodded toward their friend Ali, who carried a broom over his shoulder.

"No way," said Carol. She and Mildred shuffled to the outhouses and got to work cleaning. Outside, other kids swept up leaves or pulled weeds in the playground. Inside the main cement building, students cleaned the blackboards, desks, and floors. Teachers and prefects (PREE-fekts) supervised to make sure the work was done well.

After they finished cleaning, the kids lined up in the schoolyard for morning assembly. Girls stood on one side of the yard and boys

on the other, with the smallest kids lined up in front and the biggest in back. They all wore their school's blue-and-white uniforms. The teachers stood against the wall of the school, opposite the kids.

When everyone was in place, the headmaster made a few announcements. Six students, three girls and three boys, raised the Kenyan flag, and the whole school sang the national anthem.

After the assembly, the kids broke out of their lines and walked to their classrooms. Mildred and Carol's room had a cement floor. Students sat at rows of benches, with each desk shared among three or four people. A black-painted section of the wall served as a chalkboard, and a corkboard hung by the door. The windows

Most schools in Kenya are simple buildings with few facilities besides classrooms. The climate is warm year-round, and there is no air-conditioning, so many school buildings have no glass in the windows.

Kenyan classes tend to be very large. Kids like Mildred and her friends have to do their best to share desk space, textbooks, and attention from their teachers.

were holes in the walls with iron bars across them. A tin roof covered the building.

The 40 third graders in Mildred's class stood by their desks until Mr. Hassan greeted them and invited them to sit. Mildred yawned as the teacher began the science lesson. It was the same thing every day: science, math, social studies, **Kiswahili** (kee-swah-HEE-lee), and English. Some days they had art, PE, or religion. Kids' parents chose whether their children would learn about Christianity, **Hinduism**, or **Islam**. There was a rumor that the school would get some computers donated soon, but nobody was sure when.

Samosas

Mildred yawned again as she opened the science textbook and laid it on the desk. The school provided books, but there weren't enough, so three or four students shared each one. It was a pain, but at least the kids' families didn't have to buy them. Most families, including Mildred's, could hardly afford to buy the school uniform and basic school supplies.

At recess, some of the kids bought doughnuts or meat-filled pies called **samosas** (suh-MOH-suz). The school didn't have a cafeteria,

Some students at Mildred's school buy lunch at the school kitchen and eat on the playground.

so they lined up at the kitchen window, and a lady handed the food out to them. They ate on the playground. The snacks smelled good, but Mildred didn't have any money. She did get a cup of spiced tea, called chai (CHY), which the school gave students free.

Carol got her cup of chai and stood beside Mildred to drink it. "What's going on?" she asked.

"I'm just wishing for a little excitement," said Mildred. She looked at the sky, hoping for a rainstorm. Storms kept life interesting because the rain fell so hard on the tin roof that nobody could hear a word Mr. Hassan said. But today the sky was clear.

"I'll race you to the neem tree and back," said Carol, setting down her cup. "That could be exciting."

That wasn't what Mildred had in mind. She opened her mouth to say so, but Carol was already running.

"Come on, slowpoke!" Carol called over her shoulder. Mildred laughed and ran to catch up.

The recess cheered Mildred up a little, but math and English went as slowly as science. When lunchtime finally came, she waved to Carol and went home to eat. Her mother had cooked a mixture of corn and beans called ***githeri*** (gih-THER-ee). Kids who lived too far away to go home for lunch bought githeri from the school kitchen or walked to the market to buy candy and snacks.

Githeri

That afternoon, Mildred's class had a quiz in social studies. The kids sat quietly, concentrating on their work.

"Hey!" shouted Ali. "Get away!"

Mildred jumped and looked around, afraid that Mr. Hassan would slap Ali for shouting in the middle of the test. But Mr. Hassan was just standing with his mouth open, looking at the donkey that had somehow found its way into the classroom. It was trying to eat Ali's quiz. Ali tried to pull the quiz out of the donkey's mouth,

but the paper tore, and the donkey got the bigger piece. The class erupted into laughter.

"How did it get in here?" asked Mr. Hassan. He tried to push the donkey out the door.

"I have no idea, sir," Ali said, pulling on the rope around the donkey's neck.

The donkey wouldn't budge. It just stood still and chewed.

The quiz was abandoned, and the next fifteen minutes became an informal vacation. Kids and teachers from neighboring classrooms ran in to see what was going on. Three of the teachers, working together, finally got the donkey outside.

Mildred didn't stay after school to jump rope or play soccer with the other kids like she usually did. She just ran home, bringing her notebook, so she could study that afternoon while it was still light. At home, she found her mother stirring a pot of food and trying to comfort her crying little brother. Her mother wore many beaded necklaces that rattled when she moved.

"Thank goodness you're home," said her mother. "Can you watch this pot for a minute? And then I need you to go get some water from the well."

**Maasi women
wearing beaded jewelry**

"Sure." Mildred stirred the pot and told her mother about the donkey that got into the school. Her mother smiled as she rocked the baby.

"I wanted something exciting to happen," Mildred said. "I guess I got my wish!"

Make Your Own Bead Necklace

You Will Need
Small multicolored beads
String
Scissors
An adult to help you

Instructions
1. Cut a length of string for your necklace. Be sure to make it long enough to slip easily over your head.

2. String the first bead about three finger widths from the end of your string. Ask an adult to help you tie the string firmly around the bead. As you string more beads, the bead tied at the end will keep the rest from slipping off the string.

3. String the rest of the beads from the other end, in any order you wish.

4. When your string is almost full of beads, ask an adult to help you tie the ends together.

5. Try your necklace on, or give it to somebody you think would like it.

Thailand

Thailand's calm bays and beautiful beaches attract tourists from around the world.

Thailand

Chapter

Atom rode up to the edge of his schoolyard and parked his bike. As he passed the teacher who waited for the students by the gates, he paused to **wai** (WY) her. He put his hands together just under his chin as if he were praying. Then he bobbed his head and bowed slightly. "Good morning, teacher," he said shyly.

Atom crossed the playground, stopping to *wai* the Buddhist shrine at its edge. He entered the play area on the ground floor of the school.

"Hello!" he called to his friend Sunisa. Sunisa jumped up and ran over to him.

"What are you bringing teacher tomorrow?" she asked.

Atom clapped his hand over his mouth. "Tomorrow is Teacher's Day!" he said.

"I know." Sunisa laughed. "That's why I'm asking."

"I completely forgot. I promised my mother I'd help her this afternoon. I don't have time to get flowers."

"Time for morning assembly!" said a teacher. Before Atom and Sunisa could say any more, they got caught up in a crowd of kids. They went outside and lined up on the playground. All of them wore uniforms: white shirts and khakis for the boys, white shirts and navy blue skirts for the girls.

It was a Wednesday, the day for the weekly cleanliness inspection. Atom fidgeted as a teacher checked the children's fingernails and looked behind their ears to make sure they were

Students in Atom's class sit in long rows of desks. When their teacher enters the room, they show their respect by standing up and greeting her.

clean. He didn't know what to do about Teacher's Day tomorrow. He almost wished Sunisa hadn't reminded him. He couldn't get out of helping his mother. His uncle was visiting the following evening, and Atom knew she wanted everything to be perfect.

At exactly eight o'clock in the morning, the kids and teachers sang the Thai national anthem. A few kids who came late were still running toward the lines when the song began. They stopped wherever they were and stood still until the anthem was over.

Then it was time for school to begin. Atom ran inside with the other kids. At the foot of the stairs that led up to the classrooms,

he removed his shoes and carried them. He and his 38 classmates all left their shoes on the big rack at the door of their room. The walls of the room were bare except for a green chalkboard at the front. Teacher's big table and chair sat at the front, and rows of desks filled the rest of the space.

When Sunisa came in, she caught Atom's eye and hurried to the desk beside him. She opened her mouth to speak, but teacher entered the classroom before she had a chance to say anything.

"Students, stand up!" called the class captain.

The kids rose. "Good morning, teacher," they said in unison.

"Good morning," said teacher. She gestured that they could sit.

"Thank you, teacher," said the kids.

Atom sat down and got to work. He studied math, Thai language, and arts. Third graders like him took all of their classes in Thai, but they would begin learning English in sixth grade. There were no computers at Atom's small-town school, but he knew that schools in Thailand's big cities usually had computer rooms.

Atom's school had no recess except at midday, so Atom worked hard all morning. When lunchtime came, he was still worrying about Teacher's Day. He grabbed his lunch container full of rice and meat from home and sat down under a tree on the playground. He didn't feel like eating, and he ignored the kids playing hide-and-seek around him.

Sunisa dropped down on the ground beside him with her lunch. "I'll get enough flowers for both of us. I'll bring them by your house this evening. We can make our bouquets together."

"You will?" Atom said. "You're a lifesaver. I can't imagine what would happen if I forgot."

Atom felt better during the afternoon lessons, but his mind kept wandering to tomorrow, when all the kids would bow to the teachers and give them flowers or wreaths. It was always

Chicken fried rice and vegetables

fun to see how many flowers each child brought, and Atom knew the teachers enjoyed the attention. Some teachers took the time to give a short speech to each child, wishing him or her good luck for the rest of the school year.

"Atom!"

Atom snapped out of his daydream. "Yes, teacher?"

"I asked you to solve the next math problem."

Atom gulped, looked at his book, and guessed which problem was next. When he solved it correctly, teacher looked at him suspiciously before she nodded and moved on. Atom breathed a sigh of relief. He hadn't been paying attention, and he was lucky to get away without punishment. Teacher could have spanked him or made him stand on one foot in front of the whole class. He normally worked hard, not just because he might get punished, but also because school was expensive and his mother always told him he must.

When school was over, Atom rode his bike home and helped his mother. She asked him to wash dishes and sweep the house. Just as he was finishing, Sunisa appeared at the door with her arms full of flowers.

"Wow!" Atom said. "You got a lot."

He and Sunisa sat down and arranged their bouquets. Atom used mostly orange flowers, but Sunisa mixed all the colors together. Both of them added a few leaves around the edges.

**Big Buddha
Koh Samui**

"Thanks again for helping me," Atom said as they finished.
"No problem," said Sunisa. "It was fun."

Atom smiled as he put his bouquet by the door. He had no more worries. Tomorrow would be an excellent day.

Make Your Own Teacher's Day Bouquet

You Will Need
Flowers or leaves
String
A paper towel
Tissue paper
Ribbon
An adult to help you

In Thailand, kids make bouquets and present them to teachers every year on Teacher's Day. You can have Teacher's Day at your school, too.

Instructions
1. Ask an adult to help you find a safe place to gather flowers near your home. You could look for flowers in a local park or ask permission to pick them from gardens in your neighborhood. If you don't have flowers available nearby, gather leaves instead.

2. Arrange your flowers or leaves into a bouquet. If you think it won't stay together on its own, ask an adult to help you tie the stems loosely with a piece of string.

3. To keep your bouquet fresh, wet a paper towel and wrap it around the bottom of the stems.

4. Wrap the flowers in tissue paper and tie with a ribbon.

5. Give your bouquet to your teacher as a present.

Russia

The Cathedral of Saint Basil the Blessed in Moscow was built in 1560. Its ninth chapel was added in 1588.

Russia

Chapter

"Bye, Mama!" Natasha shut the door of her apartment building and ran down the steps. She walked the two blocks to the school, tossed her schoolbag on the ground, and joined a game of hide-and-seek on the playground. She was crouching behind a bush when she remembered her homework.

"Uh-oh," she said. She left her hiding spot and went back and looked in her schoolbag. Sure enough, she had left her notebook at home. Again.

Natasha felt her face turn red. It was too late to go back and get her book. School was starting. She entered the block building and went to the coatroom, dawdling as she hung up her things. What would Mrs. Maslova say?

Natasha's classroom was full of bright colors, with student artwork on the walls and plants in the windowsills. On one wall, Mrs. Maslova had painted a colorful mural of this year's third-grade class. But today, Natasha felt too dismal to let the bright colors cheer her up. She tugged at the long sleeves of her pink shirt as she dragged her feet to the two-person desk she shared with her best friend, Lena.

"What's wrong?" asked Lena.

"I forgot my homework again."

"That's the third time this term!" Lena said. She was dressed like any other kid, in a sweater and jeans, but her face looked stern, like a teacher's. Natasha rolled her eyes.

Mrs. Maslova came in, and the students stood up and faced the front of the room.

"Good morning, class," said Mrs. Maslova. "You may sit down." There was a racket as 26 kids pulled out their chairs.

Natasha chewed on her lower lip as Mrs. Maslova collected homework notebooks from every student except her. Then she assigned two students to hand yesterday's notebooks back. Each student had two notebooks. Every day, the kids were supposed to turn one in and do their homework in the other.

Parents at Natasha's school take pictures of their kids on the first day of the year. Natasha's teacher has decorated the room with art and plants. The students have dressed up in black and white for this special occasion.

When Natasha got yesterday's homework back, she almost groaned out loud. Her grades were poor in English and in Russian language and literature. Her scores in math and in geography and environment were fine, but she was disappointed anyway.

"Will your parents be mad?" whispered Lena, looking over Natasha's shoulder.

"They'll probably make me do extra homework," Natasha replied.

"Natasha!" said Mrs. Maslova, who did not allow any talking in class. "Since you're so chatty this morning, why don't you get up and solve the first five math problems I've written on the board?"

Natasha walked to the chalkboard. She knew Mrs. Maslova meant to punish her for talking, but it was almost a relief to do math. It took her attention off her problems.

At the first morning break, Mrs. Maslova called Natasha up to her desk to talk while the other students went outside to play soccer and tag.

"You've got to stop forgetting your work, Natasha," said Mrs. Maslova. "You're a good student when you concentrate." Then, as Natasha expected, Mrs. Maslova asked for yesterday's homework notebook. Inside it, she wrote a note to Natasha's parents about the missing work.

"I expect to see a signature from one of your parents on this tomorrow," Mrs. Maslova said.

Natasha was relieved when lunchtime came. As usual, she had a sandwich and an apple from home. She sat at a cafeteria table next to Lena, who bought some rolls and a cup of tea at the school buffet.

"Want to come over and play this evening?" asked Natasha.

Lena looked skeptical. "Will your parents let me?"

"Oh," said Natasha, remembering her homework and the note from Mrs. Maslova. "Maybe not. I'll call you if it's okay."

blintzes

That afternoon in arts and crafts, Natasha's class made nesting dolls. They used them to decorate the back corners of the classroom. After art, all the kids pitched in to help clean the room. Natasha swept the floor. Other kids watered the plants, organized the desks, and put up the chairs. Mrs. Maslova's class often won the school's contest for neatness.

Natasha's school sometimes held special assemblies, and in autumn they held an event to show the parents the crafts they made at school. On other days, they followed a steady routine, with four or five lessons every day and a ten- or fifteen-minute break after each one.

That afternoon, Natasha walked home as slowly as she could. When her father asked to see her homework notebook, she handed it over.

"You've got to be less forgetful," he said as he signed Mrs. Maslova's note. As Natasha expected, he said she had to do extra homework, and she had to start right away. Natasha sighed and opened her books. She knew she would be working for well over an hour. She called Lena to admit that she wouldn't be able to play that evening.

"Oh, well," said Lena. "I'll help you with your work in class tomorrow, okay? Then you'll be able to play tomorrow."

"If I remember my notebook," said Natasha.

"You'd better remember!" Lena said.

Natasha smiled and said goodbye. She sat down at the table and got back to work. Maybe tomorrow would turn out better.

Russian dancers

Make Your Own Russian Nesting Dolls

You Will Need
1 large plastic cup or container with lid
1 medium plastic cup or container
1 small plastic cup or container
Heavy white paper
Colorful markers
Scissors
Clear adhesive tape

Instructions

1. Make sure that each cup is empty and clean.

2. Cut a rectangular strip of heavy white paper to fit around each cup.

3. On each piece of paper, draw a round girl face, with rosy cheeks. Draw a scarf around each face. Draw the scarf tie under the girl's chin. Draw flowers and other fun designs to make her dress.

4. Next, use the colored markers to brightly color each of your drawings.

5. Once the drawings are complete, wrap each drawing around its respective cup. Be sure the cup is upside down to the drawing.

6. Attach the drawings to the cups with clear tape.

7. Now you can stack the dolls from smallest to largest. Use the lid to keep the dolls in place when they are stacked.

Senegal

Pounding millet is a common chore for both children and adults in Senegal. Many girls and women wear loose, light dresses called bubus.

Senegal

Chapter

"Come on, Aminata," said Samba. "We're going to be late."

Aminata yawned. "I don't see why I have to go to school when I'm too tired to learn."

Samba said nothing. He just quickened his pace and hoped that Aminata would keep up. He was sorry his sister felt so tired. He knew she had been awake most of the night to care for their younger sister, who was sick with diarrhea. Their mother was going to have another baby soon, so Aminata had to do most of the housework. Still, their mother insisted that Aminata go to school this morning.

Clip-clop, clip-clop. Samba turned around to see a **charette** (shuh-RET), pulled by a donkey, approaching them on the dusty road.

"Samba!" said his friend Mohammad, who was riding in the *charette* with his father. "Would you like a ride?"

"Please," Samba said. He and Aminata climbed up. Samba wiped the sweat off his face with the corner of his T-shirt. It was nice to ride instead of walking the three kilometers (almost two miles) to school.

"Are you coming to school?" asked Samba. He glanced nervously at Mohammad's father.

"I am," said Mohammad. "My father is going this way anyway, so he said he would drive me."

Mohammad's father just grunted, urging the donkey to go faster. Samba knew the man thought his son should drop out, even though school was free. He sometimes made Mohammad stay home to run errands or work in the fields.

But Mohammad insisted on staying in school. One of the smartest boys in the village, he passed his classes every year. At eleven, he was already in his sixth year. He planned to finish high school no matter what his father said.

Like many other students at their school, Samba and Aminata were behind. Aminata was twelve, but she was only in her third year of school because she often had to stay and help at home. Samba was eight, and he was repeating his first year. He had missed school for a month with **malaria** (muh-LAYR-ee-uh) the year before, so he didn't learn enough to pass his exams.

The *charette* pulled up to the concrete school with a few minutes to spare. "Thanks for the ride," Samba said to Mohammad's father as the kids climbed down. The man shrugged.

On the playground, Aminata sat down and drummed on metal barrels with some of the girls. Samba and Mohammad joined a

Samba's school building has heavy metal blinds on the windows. Students and teachers usually keep the blinds open to allow air to flow.

The students at Samba's school enjoy beating metal drums in their spare time.

soccer game. A few minutes later, a teacher beat an old metal tire rim that hung from the only tree in the yard. The students, nearly all of them barefoot, stood at attention as some older boys raised the Senegalese flag.

When the flag was up, the kids went to their classes. Samba followed the other 35 first years into his bare-walled classroom. Before the lessons began, he helped to adjust the tin blinds in the glassless windows to make sure the air was blowing through. The breeze would keep the room cool during the lessons. Samba took his seat at one of the wooden benches.

Madame Dior began the day by reviewing the French phrases the class was supposed to have memorized the day before. When it was Samba's turn to recite in front of everyone, he felt his palms sweat. He liked writing answers much better than speaking in front of the class. As he recited, he glanced nervously at the stick propped on Madame Dior's desk. Sometimes she hit the students with it when they made mistakes, but today Samba didn't mess up.

As a first-year student, Samba mostly learned French. Like everyone else in the village, he spoke **Wolof** (WOH-lof) at home. He had to learn French before he could go on to higher grades

In Senegalese classrooms, students of different ages often study together. Illnesses, chores, and family events often keep them from progressing steadily through school.

and learn other subjects. Older kids, he knew, learned things like math and science, the history of Senegal, and world history. They also studied writing and singing, **hygiene** (HY-jeen), and civic duty.

Samba wanted to do well in school, but it was hard. He had been healthy enough to study every day this year, but Madame Dior was often absent. When she was gone, sometimes another teacher tried to teach two classes—60 or 70 kids—at once, but sometimes there was no school at all. Samba knew he wasn't learning as much as he should.

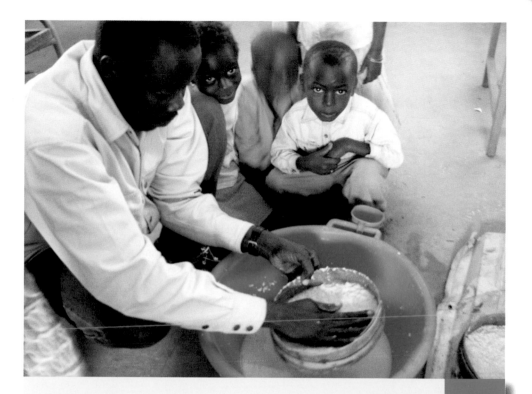

Students and teachers at Samba's school work together to make millet porridge.

After their recitations, the students went outside for morning break. Samba, who hadn't eaten breakfast, was happy to get some sweet **millet** (MIL-it) porridge from the village woman whose turn it was to cook for the students. Then he ran around with the other kids. After the break, as they were filing back into their classrooms, Samba saw a familiar darkness in the sky.

"Sandstorm!" he shouted.

Everyone rushed inside. Samba and his classmates shut the blinds quickly before the storm arrived. There were no electric lights in the classroom, so they couldn't work on reading and writing. Madame Dior tried to get the class to recite French phrases, but nobody could hear well above the howling wind and rattling

Chebujen

blinds. Sand blew in, dusting the benches and the concrete floor. When the wind died down, everybody pitched in to sweep up the mess.

At lunchtime, Samba got to eat **chebujen** (cheb-YOO-jen), rice with fish and vegetables. A woman served it in big bowls. Five or six students sat around each bowl on the floor, eating the food with their hands. They hauled water to drink from one of the village wells. They had no running water, but they were lucky to have a brand-new outhouse. Last year, everyone had to go to the bathroom in the fields near the school.

bubu

The building grew very hot during afternoon lessons, and Samba was glad when they were finally dismissed. He met Aminata outside the building. The light, colorful dress she was wearing, called a **bubu** (BOO-boo), fluttered in the wind. She had a rare smile on her face.

"Guess what?" she said. "Amadou's older sister is getting married. We're going to have a wedding next week!"

Samba grinned too. Weddings made great parties, with food, drumming, and dancing.

"I have to go home and cook dinner," Aminata said, still smiling. "Be sure to practice your French verbs."

"I will," said Samba. He spent the afternoon climbing mango trees with some other boys. On his way home for dinner, he tried to practice reciting his lesson, but he wasn't sure he remembered it correctly.

"Can you help me with my French?" he asked Aminata as he entered their hut. His sister was rocking the sick child and stirring the *chebujen*. His mother lay in the corner.

"I'll try to help after we eat." Aminata yawned. Samba waited as she fed the family and cleaned up, but she fell asleep as soon as she was finished.

Samba sighed and recited his lesson in his head as well as he could remember it. He knew he was making mistakes, but he did the best he could. Before he got to the end, he fell asleep, too.

Senegal *djun djun* drums

Make Your Own African Drum

You Will Need
A coffee can with lid
Scissors
Construction paper
Crayons or colored markers
Glue

Instructions
1. Cut a piece of construction paper to fit around the outside of your container.

2. Decorate the paper with African designs.

3. Cover the back of the construction paper with an even layer of glue, and glue it around the outside of your drum container.

4. Put the lid on, and enjoy beating your drum!

Rural Alaska

The northern lights, also known as the aurora borealis, often light the Alaskan sky at night.

Rural Alaska

Chapter

Sarah ran down the sidewalk and then stopped abruptly, sliding on her shoes across the ice. The streetlights shone down on her friend Mary, who slid on the ice ahead of her. The two girls laughed, their voices muffled by their scarves.

It was still dark as the girls walked to school. In winter, the days in their part of Alaska were short. The sun would come out for only a few hours during the day. But a few months from now, in summer, it would be light outside almost all the time.

The two girls rounded the corner and ran up the stairs to the school. The building was raised on stilts because the ground underneath was **permafrost** (PUR-muh-frost), which could get spongy in warm weather.

They entered the building through the **Elders** Hall, a big room the school used as a cafeteria and assembly area. Murals on the walls displayed pictures of all the village elders. As always, Sarah glanced proudly at her grandfather's picture as she walked by. When they arrived in their classroom, Sarah and Mary stripped off their parkas, boots, and snow pants. They hung them in their cubbies.

"You have a new *kuspuk!*" said Sarah. She stood back to admire the long, hooded shirt with pockets that Mary was wearing over her jeans. It was made from flowered cloth, and it flared out at the bottom like a skirt. Lots of the grown-up women in town wore *kuspuks*, but Sarah didn't have one.

At the beginning of their school day, Sarah and her friends talk and laugh with each other until their teacher tells them to go to their desks.

Sarah and Mary talked and joked with their classmates. They were all standing around when the bell rang to signal the start of the day.

"Good morning, everyone!" Miss Rasmussen said loudly. She stood with her hands folded in front of her, staring around the room. Slowly, her 22 students stopped talking and went to sit at their desks.

Mary led the Pledge of Allegiance, and then Miss Rasmussen started the social studies lesson. The class also studied reading, math, and science, as well as Sarah's favorites, art and PE.

Almost everyone in Sarah's town was part of a southwestern Alaskan Eskimo tribe called the **Yupik** (YOO-pik) people. Classes were taught in the Yupik language from kindergarten to second grade. But now that they were in third grade, Sarah and her friends studied in English. They were still supposed to have a Yupik class, but the school couldn't find a Yupik teacher for the older grades this year.

When she first moved to Alaska from North Dakota, Miss Rasmussen didn't know much about Yupik culture. For the Yupik people, raised eyebrows mean "yes," and a wrinkled nose means "no." Miss Rasmussen once confessed that before she knew this, she wondered if the kids all thought she smelled bad!

It was very cold outside that day, so Sarah's class went to the gym for recess. As usual, everybody wanted to play basketball. The gym was so crowded that it was hard to get a game going.

"I have an idea," said Sonny. "All girls get off the court!"

"That's not fair!" said Sarah, who loved basketball. When Sonny wouldn't change his mind, Sarah got so mad she pushed him.

"Sarah," warned Miss Rasmussen.

"Sorry." Sarah looked down at the floor.

"When I get back, I want to see both boys and girls playing a game," said Miss Rasmussen. To Sarah, she added, "Come with me."

Sarah followed Miss Rasmusen back to the classroom. Miss Rasmussen pointed to a chair, and Sarah sat in it. "How would your grandfather feel if he knew you got angry and pushed someone?" the teacher asked.

To be polite, Sarah kept her eyes turned away from Miss Rasmussen's face. "I guess he wouldn't like it," she whispered.

After that, Sarah worried all through reading. Would Miss Rasmussen tell Sarah's grandfather what she had done? Like most of the elders, he

Steamed crab

came to the Elders Hall to join the students every day for lunch. Luckily, Miss Rasmussen didn't tell. When Sarah waved hello to her grandfather at lunchtime, he smiled at her just as warmly as always.

Sarah picked up her plastic tray of chicken nuggets and canned green beans, and she went to eat with Mary. Like most of their classmates at their free public school, Sarah and Mary were on the free lunch plan. The part of Alaska where they lived was quite poor. There were no roads between towns because it was impossible to build them on the permafrost. It was hard for grown-ups to find jobs, and store-bought food cost a lot of money because it all had to be brought in airplanes. At home, Sarah's family ate mostly food they caught and gathered themselves, such as crabs, seal, salmon, moose, and berries.

Unlike students in other parts of the United States, kids in Sarah's school never went on field trips. The whole class would have had to fly in a plane just to get to a museum. But sometimes people traveled from out of town to hold job fairs or assemblies at the school.

It was a Wednesday, so Sarah went to practice in a traditional dance group after school. Most other days she played basketball at the gym or went home to watch TV. If her big brother James was in a good mood, he occasionally took her **ice fishing** or **snow machining**. In Sarah's opinion, gliding across the snow on a snow machine was one of the best feelings in the world. It almost made up for living in a town with no movie theater.

At the end of the day, Sarah trudged home in the dark. She kicked the snow off her boots before she went inside.

Yupik dancer

"Hi, Sarah," said her mom. "Did you have a good day?"

"Just normal." Sarah pulled off her boots.

"Normal for you, maybe," said Sarah's mother. "But some people might think it was extraordinary."

Make Your Own Inuksuk (Or More than One Inuksuit)

The native people of Alaska and northern Canada used to make human-shaped structures called inuksuit out of stones. An inuksuk could mark a meeting place, help people find their way through unfamiliar land, or convey messages. Some inuksuit also held spiritual meanings.

You Will Need

Many flat-sided stones
A flat, safe place to build
An adult to help you

Instructions

1. Ask an adult to help you find a good place, such as a backyard or a local park, to gather rocks you can use to build an inuksuk. Look for rocks that are flat on two sides. They may range in size, but you will need several large ones about the size of your fist.

2. With your adult helper, choose a flat work space for building your inuksuk.

3. Arrange your rocks into the shape of a person. It is best to start with the largest rocks and then place smaller rocks on top. If necessary, use very small rocks as wedges to keep larger rocks balanced.

FURTHER READING

Books

Ajmera, Maya, and Anna Rhesa Versola. *Children from Australia to Zimbabwe: A Photographic Journey Around the World.* Watertown, Massachusetts: Charlesbridge, 2001.

UNICEF. *A Life Like Mine: How Children Live Around the World.* New York: DK Publishing, 2005.

UNICEF. *A School Like Mine: A Unique Celebration of Schools Around the World.* New York: DK Publishing, 2007.

Acknowledgments

This book is based on the author's interviews throughout 2008 and 2009 with people who have firsthand experience in schools around the world. The author would like to thank the following people who donated their time, experience, and thoughtful insights to the project:

Alaska: Antara Brewer taught in Kipnuk. Susanna Mishler visited schools in the Yupiit School District (Tuluksak, Akiak, Akiachak) and Napakiak.

Costa Rica: Ashley Ann Baker worked at Centro Educativa Térraba in Térraba de Buenos Aires. David Larkin worked at Escuela José Joaquín Mora Porras, Government Housing Project of Jireth, El Roble, Puntarenas. Daniel Merin worked at Escuela Los Lirios de Puerto Limón. All three were Peace Corps volunteers.

Finland: Heidi Maria Kuusela attends Raunistula School in Turku. Akseli Pullinen attends Savonlinnan normaalikoulu in Savonlinna; his family also helped answer some questions. Wilhelmina Ojanen attends Amuri School in Tampere.

Kenya: Libby Bryant worked at Tumutumu School for the Deaf in the village of Tumutumu. Adam Diehl taught at Faza Secondary School near the Kenya/Somali border. Anne McGrath taught at Lugala Primary School in Shinyalu. Erickson Young worked at Kichakamkwaju Unit for the Deaf in Shimoni, Coast Province. All four were Peace Corps volunteers.

Russia: Svetlana Knyazeva spent her early school years in the town of Nizhnij Arkhyz; her family was also helpful in answering questions.

FURTHER READING

Senegal: Megan Hansen worked as a Peace Corps volunteer at Ngekhokh Elementary School, in the village of Ngekhokh.
Thailand: Jintana Suktavee grew up in Thailand and attended Bhanchantaklem School in Chantaburi.
Turkey: Megan Dryden taught at Çakabey Schools in Izmir.

Thanks, also, to the many people who provided advice or helped make connections with interviewees, especially Laurie Koosmann, Minna Vaisanen, Megan Hansen, Nan Breuninger, and Andy Breuninger.

The following web site was also helpful in preparing this book:

Barrow, Richard. "A Day in a Thai School." Accessed February 10, 2009. http://www.thaischoollife.com/day-at-school.html

On the Internet
Around the World in 80 Schools.
> http://www.aroundtheworldin80schools.com/
> Watch videos and see pictures of teacher Charline Evans's amazing trip to see 80 different schools around the world.

Cool Planet. http://www.oxfam.org.uk/coolplanet/kidsweb/wakeup/index.htm
> Find out about the daily lives of kids in four different countries.

Students of the World. http://www.studentsoftheworld.info/
> Look up websites for schools and find pen-pals from countries around the world.

Time for Kids: Around the World.
> http://www.timeforkids.com/TFK/kids/hh/goplaces
> Read facts about history, sightseeing, and life in dozens of countries.

GLOSSARY

Words from foreign languages appear in *italic*.

bubu (BOO-boo)—A colorful, airy dress worn by some girls and women in Senegal and other parts of Africa.

charette (shuh-RET)—A wooden cart pulled by a horse or donkey.

chebujen (cheb-YOO-jen)—Rice with fish and vegetables.

elders (EL-durs)—Older people; people who deserve respect.

fast—A period of time during which a person chooses not to eat food, usually as part of a religious act.

geometric (jee-oh-MEH-trik)—Having regular shapes.

githeri (gih-THER-ee)—A mixture of corn and beans.

Hinduism (HIN-doo-iz-um)—A religion that comes from India.

hygiene (HY-jeen)—Practicing healthy habits such as bathing and toothbrushing.

ice fishing—Fishing through a hole in ice.

inuksuit (ih-NUK-soo-it)—Two or more inuksuk.

inuksuk (ih-NUK-suk)—A human-shaped landmark made out of stone by people in northern Alaska or Canada.

Islam (IZ-lahm)—The Muslim religion.

Kiswahili (kee-swah-HEE-lee)—One of the two official languages of Kenya.

kofta (KOOF-tuh)—A spicy meatball, often made with lamb.

kuspuk (KUS-puk)—A long-sleeved, hooded shirt with pockets that is worn by some Yupik people.

malaria (muh-LAYR-ee-uh)—A serious sickness spread by mosquitoes.

millet (MIL-it)—A kind of grain.

mosaic (moh-ZAY-ik)—A picture made of many small, colorful pieces.

neem tree—A tropical tree that is common in Kenya.

permafrost (PUR-muh-frost)—Ground that is frozen or partly frozen all year round.

Ramadan (RAH-muh-dahn)—A Muslim holy month.

samosa (suh-MOH-suh)—A kind of meat or vegetable pie.

snow machining—Riding a snow machine or snowmobile.

soda (SOH-dah)—A small store that sells snacks and drinks.

unison (YOO-nih-sun)—At the same time.

wai (WY)—A Thai greeting.

Wolof (WOH-lof)—A language of Senegal.

Yupik (YOO-pik)—A southwest Alaskan people. Along with the Inuit and the Aleut, they make up the group that is sometimes called Eskimos.

INDEX

ABOUT THE AUTHOR

Melissa Koosmann studied creative writing at Linfield College and at the University of Arizona. After spending a few years teaching writing classes and tutoring college students with learning disabilities, she decided to become a full-time freelance writer. Melissa has traveled extensively around the world, visiting almost twenty different countries—including Kenya and Costa Rica, two of the countries profiled in this book. Since 2008, she has been living with her husband in Cape Town, South Africa. When she is not exploring South Africa and having adventures, she spends most of her time writing and tutoring at a local elementary school.